CW00485640

The boy who couldn't say his name

JOHN LAWRENCE

V.

Published in the United Kingdom in 2019
by V. Press,
10 Vernon Grove,
Droitwich,
Worcestershire,
WR9 9LQ.

ISBN: 978-1-9998444-5-5

Copyright © John Lawrence, 2019.

The right of John Lawrence to be identified as the author of this work has been asserted by him in accordance with the Copyrights, Designs and Patents Act of 1988. All rights reserved. No part of this publication may be reproduced, stored in a retrieval system, transmitted in any form or by any means, electronic, photocopying, recording or otherwise, without prior permission of the publisher.

Cover design © Ruth Stacey, 2019.

Printed in the U.K. by Imprint Digital, Seychelles Farm, Upton Pyne, Exeter EX5 5HY, on recycled paper stock.

Acknowledgements

There's a long trail of people to thank, some of whom may not realise how invaluable their support has been: starting with the creative writing tutors at the University of Birmingham, who saw potential when I couldn't. Also, the Worcestershire area's writers and performers, for their unwavering support. Many thanks to the members of the Poetry Society's Worcestershire Stanza group, past and present, whose honest feedback and encouragement has been invaluable. Thanks particularly to my 'buddy' group, Sarah James, Kathy Gee and Jenna Plewes, for their never-failing ability to restore my self-belief, and to all at V Press, for their hard work, support and wise words. And finally, to my wife Liz, for always being there and for not questioning my sanity when catching a glimpse of my poems' first drafts.

V.

Contents

V.

V.

For Elizabeth

V.

V.

Boundary News

[handwritten: Start in dis.]

The fence between our neighbouring ground
has slipped into disrepair. I stand and think

how long this has been going on. The posts
are rotting, winter rains washing them away

until the cycle is complete, atom by atom;
it will not slow when spring idles in.

A fire would speed it up, but the overgrowth
and nurtured land might suffer. I know

[handwritten: mile brews]

creatures shuttle day and night along the boundary
ridge, using their claws to grip their right of way,

hastening the decay. I seldom see the man next door;
his curtains stay three-quarters shut; he burns candles

for his creed and when we meet he can only talk
of his preferred certainty, not of everyday tasks

like fixing a fence. I have to do this alone.
With sturdy gloves and long-handled axe,

I'll show what's got to be done and bring him
to his senses. It will be a small victory.

[handwritten: .. still stuff I've seen b4.
do more Ocean mags!]

7

The Family Chess Set

The unfolded board shows a split down the centre
from a lifetime of opening and closing.
I gather the pieces around the edge, massed

for the battle. When ready, I want a slow
and easy ingress, to recite their names,
question each piece about intentions

before I release them into the field.
On a white bishop's shoulder,
a nick hacked out after a revenge attack

with a protractor; the black queen, her beauty
enhanced by a blob of Tipp-Ex on her crown.
Two mercenary pawns are still missing

in action, one from each side, their power
always downplayed and easily dismissed
by the fools in the upper ranks.

Solid in the four corners: a reliability
of rooks, the most recusant of pieces,
in no need of the bishops' gods. I watch a knight

fly its ragged course, a reckless loner
hoping for off-guard foes.
I cannot help but think of the pain

while mourning the queen who suffered
a brutal death when mauled by pawns
in the blur of a long-ago battle.

I want to end this, to lay my fingertips
on the head of each king, treat them like crystal,
for the game without them is worthless.

Reflections

skimming stones

You'd skim the stones
on the flat of the bay, pleased
with one, two, three, four skips;

turn to me with that lopsided smile.
I'd nod and wave to spur you on,
watch as you sought the perfect stone,

bounced it in your palm to test the weight.
I take some comfort that you'd only skim
when I was with you, perhaps.

Now, years on, I want to seek
my own perfect stone,
but cannot bring myself to bend.

In the space of a sigh
a fish breaks the water's skin
to gasp, or grasp an unwary fly,

then in the blink of an eye
it's the merest flutter of ripples,
like your stone's skip on the flat of the bay.

Poetry in Motion

I like a poem that tweaks my heartbeat.
I like small, perfectly placed silences
in which an image can form,
sounds that play together,
lie easily with each other,
drill the depths and earn their right.

I like a poem which accompanies my step
to a place I've never been.
A window to the world,
a window not so hard to open,
with glass that's not too cloudy.
It connects me with reality,
gives me a surprise around each corner.
A poem that's like a swan on water –
at first I see the swan
then the ripples spreading out;
I sense its feet, easing back and forth

and yet I don't feel compelled to take up time
asking why and how the swan can move
and where it's going, where it's come from.
I don't feel the urge to catch it, flail it, skin it,
to search through the entrails until my hands are bloodied
and the swan is no longer a swan.
All I want is to enjoy the sight, the sound,
and let it furiously peck at my legs
if that's what it wants to do.

Hide

In matching North Face jackets
they sit side by side, still as herons,
talking in whispers as if a lovers' tryst.

He: a single-handed hold
on an up-market scope,
one eye on the birds,
the other tightly shut.
She: two hands grip binoculars
as though they hold a secret;
scuffed and chipped
but doing the job.

On the fringe of the wetland,
two grebes declare themselves,
shake heads, ready
for their elaborate tango.

In the hide, she touches his arm,
code for *have you seen?*
He thinks of her in that blue cotton dress
at the dance where they met,
and nods his head.
This is no awkward silence,
this is it. Their safe word is teashop.

Not what they dreamed of,
but it'll do.

12

Running

Our treadmill sits in the spare room, where a bed
could go. The reasons why we bought it
are long forgotten — maybe some irrational

burst of Lycra-based zeal, but now it looks
stranded, in a corner, a contraption
without a cause. I step on and set

the destination — twenty miles, starting
slowly, with unplanned changes of gear
and gradient. I'll watch the numbers

blazing ahead, mile after sticky mile.
I can't afford to skip a beat, the unfailing
metronomic rhythm of left and right.

Imaginary crowds will line my route,
hushed as monks, a cast of faces bearing smiles
or frowns, some with heads turned, looking back

to where I began. You will be there,
half-hidden, walking away, as my run
becomes a trudge. I step off again –

by the end, my trusty GPS watch
would tell me I've stood still for all that time.

DIY and Me

Fixing things, hammering, screwing,
putting up a shelf, painting, mending.
If I had to choose between
poking red hot skewers in my eyes
or a day doing DIY,
give me those skewers every time.

Last year in June, a tap starts to leak;
a constant regular drip drip drip
drives us flippin' mad for weeks and weeks.
It takes me six months of wifely hints
to borrow a spanner from the widow next door,
then with a pencil behind one ear
I open up the tap to fix it

and see *oh crap!* no chance of a single task
a simple change of washer
as my fingers grasp this   spindle thing
a brass   spindle thing
with ridges and joins and strange-shaped holes
but I pull myself together
mustn't make a fuss
and take this   spindle thing to Plumbers R Us
where the men from The Trade buy their stuff.

I join the queue, trying to stand like a plumber,
me, the newcomer, lined up behind real men,
wearing real men's overalls, laughing real men's laughs,
smelling of putty and solder and mould-free silicone;
men who could keep a barbecue hot with their right hand
while clutching a lager in the left;
men who don't drink skinny decaf latte with just one shot.

They're talking real men's talk
with the stony-faced chap behind the well-worn counter,
asking for loops, reducers, brass tees, boiler mounts
and a close-coupled separator.
As a huge fan of close-coupling, my ears prick up,
but then the chat moves on to brass cocks and feed elbows
and all the time they keep straight faces.

Now you ought to know I'm not a bad guy
I don't go around stamping on hamsters
but it's all a bit of a haze
I feel like a fish out of water
like Ricky Gervais on Songs of Praise,
and I stand gripping my   spindle thing
as a noobie in plumbing and a bit of a wuss
the stony-faced chap beckons me forward
and I lean on the counter in real man style
and tell him about the drip drip drip
and he flippin' well asks me *what sort of tap?*

and I cry a bit
and he sighs and frowns and asks
crosstap, lever, cruciform, high-rise?

and I cry some more and feel like a prat
and I say *it's a tap!*
and he shrugs and smiles and says
what you need is a spline, mate.

Now I'm mightily thankful
not about the spline but because he's called me mate!

Then the real men turn, distracted,
forget their brass cocks and feed elbows,

and recite as one,
Oh yeah, mate, what you need is a spline.

Losing the pencil from behind my ear,
I vigorously nod as if I've always known

but I'm on cloud nine as I pay my eight quid,
madly drive home like a white van man
and fit my spline, then send a text to my wife at work:
*Fixed it, dear, it was fine, worry no more about drips,
it was, as I thought, the spline.*
And later she comes home and is filled with awe
as I chat about brass cocks and feed elbows,
yet not so much about the close-coupled separator.

Now hear me out, for in my defence at this time,
few of those real men with pencils behind ears
could write a poem with unforced rhymes,
could pen a sonnet about the colour yellow
or a villanelle about a big brown cello
or a sestina on the history of Nantucket
or a limerick ending with...
anything you like

and none of them would know:
18 words rhyme with orange,
17 with Bromsgrove,
2 with pubic,
1 with mollusc,
and nothing rhymes with wasp. Ha!

So I think I can live without D.I.Y.
I think I can live *not* knowing
a 9-mil brass male nipple when I see one

because I'm happy to sit, pen
behind my ear, sipping my skinny decaf latte
with just one shot, like the wuss that I am.

The Lament of the Zanussi Luminary

He arrives one day late,
sporting a fifty-quid-an-hour grin,
chipping the front door with his toolbox
on the way in.
Show me the beast, says he,
ah! there she is! A model 403A.
Surprised it's lasted this long,
made in Romania, y'see.

Heaving the appliance away from the wall,
arse-crack peeking inquisitively
over his Tesco Fair Trade jeans,
he hums variations on a theme from Abba,
then a string of *ahas* and *hmmms*
and words that bounce around the kitchen
from their parallel universe:
fitted clamps, drum axles, spin-gauges,
the language of man and machine
in implausible harmony.

After pointing out *yer problem*
with the tip of his B&Q screwdriver,
he talks about the hazards of life after death,
how he'd fix global warming,
how he'd make an ark if he had to,
and the creatures he wouldn't let on:

badgers, stoats, egrets,
boy bands, synchronised swimmers,
Muslims, Jews, Christians, Wolves fans,
the French and the Germans and Vladimir Putrid,
bloody poets, the makers of sun-dried tomatoes,

the exponents of Yin & Yang...
and others I couldn't make out
through the echo,
as his head was now in the drum.

Cash-in-greasy-hand, chipping the front door
on the way out, he calls himself *solid-as-a-rock*,
laments how *people don't bother any more*,
how he *can't stand today's lack of tolerance*,
and that *it's so sad.*

Who Do You Think You Are?

(Who Do You Think You Are? is a series of TV documentaries in which celebrities trace their ancestors. The producers make the celebrity visit people and places and won't let up until they sob like a beauty queen.)

Celia has discovered that her dad
was a gorilla named Grant, says she always
wondered how her arms got so long and why
she has this thing for bananas and nuts,

so Celia is on her way to see Stan,
a long-lost third cousin, who turns out
to be a bastard in more ways than one.
Family records will show that truth,
in such a graceful, sibylline hand
(an *erm* in the box where *father* should be).
Then she learns that her granny's great-uncle's son
invented apricot jam in 1903,

so Celia is taken to visit the Museum
of Apricot Jam in Thrapston,
where her granny's great-uncle's son
is immortalised in bronze on a plinth,
holding aloft an apricot and spoon,
his burnished smile shrouding the shame
that he and Mother Teresa were lovers
and once had a child, a lad named Bobo,

so Celia is now going to visit
the bungalow of a distant niece,
with her crisp white hair and M&S blouse
and a photo of a chimp on the sideboard;
they hug and smile, compare ears and noses,
nibble at carefully plated rich tea biscuits,

wow! at blanched photos of long-dead kids
in bare feet and no trace of furry hands,

so Celia is now on her way to see
the nephew of her grandmother's sister,
who lives in a flat in Berwick-upon-Tweed
with his cat called Malcolm and a collection
of labels from jars of apricot jam
(plus an array of guns in the attic)
and they sit and chat over rich tea biscuits,
frowning at pictures of folks they don't know.

Celia is sat in a caff with her hubby
as the ancestral journey sinks in.
There's no hint of a prince, lady or earl,
not even a benevolent dictator –
her tree is festooned with nothing more
than screwballs, apes and turds.
She forces a smile, turns,
and starts to groom her mate.

How truth can hurt a fish

I didn't know I was a fish
until last Friday. It came as a shock
and I wish they'd told me before.

I always thought our home
was a bit on the damp side,
that dinners were quite samey,
that we weren't a family who chatted together much,
that forgetting birthdays was normal,
that my relatives and friends
always looked surprised to see me.

It's just the way it is, I thought.

Then, last week, I was led away
by the fin,
told the truth
about who I really was.

And I'll make no bones about it,
I was bloody gutted.

Learn a lot about someone
via clutter.

Inventory: in my shed I have the following

wall-to-wall cobwebs with one humongous spider
a Betamax cassette of Easy Rider

a smallish tub of what might be earwax
one crumpled demand for unpaid poll tax

one length of rope with a sturdy knot
the mildewed remains of a fold-down cot

one broken thermometer stuck on five degrees C
one chock-full money-box without a key

one garden rake, handle whittled to a point
a Charles and Di ashtray with a half-smoked joint

eight mint copies of Practical Householder
one worn Playboy in a discreet blue folder

one dusty hockey stick together with a ball
a picture of you pinned up on the wall

one fly, trapped in a bell jar's dome
one brass weight from a broken metronome

a collection of meteorites in padded boxes
one picture of a beagle being slaughtered by foxes

one half of a two-piece snooker cue
two Away Day savers from Cheltenham to Crewe

a photo of our wedding day, faded yet intact
a blackbird's egg, hairline cracked

23

a tarnished handle from our Allegro's door
an imagined silhouette of me on the floor

the click-click-clack of a magpie up above
the silence of a life without your love

a sharpened knife lying close to hand
an hourglass timer, without any sand

Ladybird

As I peek through the gaps in the lattice fence
I see your face; you are looking back at me
from your seat in the park. There are tears

on your cheeks, which you do not brush away.
Your raise your hand to your lips
and blow me a kiss; there are many reasons

why I can't respond, many reasons
why I should not be here. Your perfection
draws me to you, still. Now, close to my head,

a ladybird walks a ridge, senses my shadow,
senses my breath, before opening its wings
and flying to you. All I can do

is stand here and wish,
wish I was with you
on that seat in the park.

Their Place

This is their place. Rented
from some sharp-toothed abuser
with a handshake as limp as a well-thumbed IOU;
he makes light of the weeping anaglypta,
the leaching sewage. Their place
is taking its time to mature while they swig
lukewarm Lambrusco from plastic cups.
They no longer sense the smell of curry
nosing up through floorboards,
seeking skin-thin erosions of carpet.

Above, on the seventies light shade
backed by the cloud-shaped stain,
a spider clambers its drift of scaffolding
while they fuck to the reassuring riffs
of Muse's City of Delusion, as the WHSmith
rent book burrows deep inside the uncomplaining sofa;
the silk flowers nod in a boot-sale vase,
dots of grey dust skip up
like hopeful pollen in a helpful breeze.

Outside their window, across their street,
over the rhythm of traffic, a windowcleaner
with windowcleaning in his genes
whistles some sassy ramshackle tune
to the frothy slap of leather on glass
as he quizzes his reflected universe
and nudges aside a twisted hood of ivy.
A dog barks in Morse code at the foot of his ladder
then lopes off to crap thoughtfully by a bus shelter
where a pale pregnant woman leans
on freshly engraved perspex, strokes her unborn child,

wonders if it can tap into her dreams
that scavenge ahead like cats in an alley.

And back in their place the landscape's the same
as the spider digests a fly. Beyond their walls
a pigeon lies on a slab of tarmac,
dreams of flying as it tries in vain
to raise its head, eyes tracking the fat red trickle
threading towards the gutter.

Spin

Inside your head, solitude is a maybe;
you sit on the clifftop, listening to the waves,
hour after hour, searching for the day
without a yesterday, or a voice
from a stranger. Now and again
the briefest whisper makes you look up –
it's only the dust settling on a rock
and you turn back to the book
cradled in your palm.

The book is about love and its spin.
Both up, both down, they have love, they have hate;
he, she, love, hate.
They walk side by side holding hands –
one and one is two plus,

or they walk alone, different directions,
opposite spin, one here, one there,
the plus is gone at the speed of light

and you are still listening to the waves
hour after hour waiting for the plus
and the faintest of sounds
in the great silence,
until the ground crumbles beneath your feet
and now you are only part of the dust
settling on a rock.

Still Life

In the lead-crystal fruit bowl
a single bullet
copper and silver
with a soft rainbow glint
pressing the skin of an apple

A child who's barely table-height
ledges her fingertips on the edge
chin resting on the wood
stares wide-eyed at the bullet
and tries to think of words to ask why

She reaches out a hand
and nudges the bullet
to pit hard into the flesh
before grabbing the apple
and inspecting its bruise

She takes a bite
from the unblemished side
the only sound is the gentle crunch
as she watches the bullet
refracted through the glass of the bowl

Outside
someone is calling a child's name
over and over again

My Father's Cap

My father's edge-worn Sally Army cap
rests in a box at the back of the wardrobe,
surviving every clear-out.

It hung on a hook in the hall
of my childhood home,
part of the backdrop,

except on Sundays, when it was worn
or carried all day. And God,
did he look the part. Smart

as can be, walking tall,
his straight-backed stride longer
than when in civvies.

The day the kids at school find out
I'm Sally Army, I show them blood
but little fire. They vent their fury

at my deceit: this kid deserves
an extra slap. Bruises the colour
of my father's cap. Many years on,

with him long gone, I brush away
the dust and our DNA, run
my fingertips around the curve

of the headband, rub at tarnish
on his badge and think of the sunlight
filtered through the stained glass

of our front-door window,
reflecting rainbows off the brass
onto that grey anaglypta wall.

As I lay his cap back in its box,
I hear myself whispering
I know
I know
I know

treat

He sits in his armchair, amid a faint smell
of damp laundry and chicken soup. Probate forms
lie untouched at his feet. He turns the mattress
every day, in her memory; sometimes he frets
that they hadn't kissed lips in twenty years.
He has his chair, TV on a stand,
an empty magazine rack. Enough, his world,
as dust-free as he can make it, all photos of her
in a shoe box in a drawer, secured
with that sturdy elastic band.
He wears a suit to go to the shops,
the only way to do it: marching tall to town,

but on his return, he flinches at his cowardice
for not stepping into traffic on the ring road.
Too often he thinks of the war in forty-four
when he lost his hearing, his mates, his innocence
to that tanned whore with her inventive style.
During the night he clearly hears gunshots
or the growl of tanks or the shouted warning
of an incoming threat; he senses the wetness
of blood-soaked cloth pressed to his skin,
or the stench of rotting flesh. And in the morning
there's the disappointment of waking,
yet another day of silent surrender.

A Prelude, of sorts

Six months from the day my fingertips
first brushed the piano keys, I can sight-read.
No small feat, it seems, as I shamble

through something resembling Chopin
with its reckless skirmishes in minor key.
Nocturnes are best, a consolation of notes:

broken chords on the left, floating melody
yearning for attention on the right.
I try to remain faithful to the form,

feel anxious when venturing into forbidden
octaves and in pieces that don't resolve,
ending as though there is no ending.

I lean on the last key to stress, feel it through hammer,
string and damper – listen, listen, newly born,
let it freely bounce around the walls

and in that moment, nothing matters but the sound,
struck fortissimo, diminuendo, subsumed
as dolce in the fabric of the room.

Nearby, someone is listening:
the woman next door,
queen of the plastic gnomes.

She sings to her cat, her notes meeting
mine in the cavity of our party wall.
Out in the street she might stammer a greeting

in her mottled voice, then blush, finger
the top button of her blouse, always.
I try to be upbeat – she sees through me,

and hurries away to the shops at a pace,
her worn-down heels clicking scales on the path.
At night if I listen hard, I imagine

a cat's purr as she smooths her hand
over its fur; the ecstasy of touch.
She doesn't know I can hear her sobs

through our wall – pianissimo, sotto.
I can't quite master Chopin's last few bars,
written as staccato, detached and abrupt,

but I linger, drawing each note
to a natural end,
like a kiss.

The Tick

Once found, it would be wrong to dig it out,
for fear of leaving its head.

The tick is fat with my blood, so in a sense
is part of me.

In time, it will drop off, start
a search for something new.

Yet I can't leave it to drink and sleep,
that may bring something worse.

The pain is fleeting; I drop the tick
in alcohol to stop it dead.

But I can see the legs still moving,
swimming for its life.

Repository

There are many people stored here,
spread around the building in trays
and drawers. A father's arms,
a daughter's hands…all unclaimed.

I'll stop thinking about them soon, I promise.

There are hearts, most likely in a vault
of their own, away from the brains
with their neurons of love or hate –
surely they'd hate if they could.

I'll stop thinking about them soon, I will.

There are tongues, no longer able
to plead or pray or scream. And now
I'm wondering where the rights and wrongs
are kept. In a soundproofed room, perhaps…

I'll stop thinking about them soon, maybe.

A room that looks empty, no visible signs
of anyone who cares, next to a door
marked Despair. Hope is stored elsewhere,
off-site, guarded, where they'd shoot you

just for thinking about it.

fractured body

(In New York, there is a repository of thousands of body parts from the World Trade Center 9/11.)

Tissue Woman

Of course you might turn your head
(that sensible charitable head)
as if hoping for the plausible distraction
of a pedestrian bouncing off a car
and pirouetting grandly into oblivion
or a banner on a bus promising
freedom from high-interest loans –
instead, your eyes turn away from her,
rest upon a scribbled shopping list
writhing and snapping in the breeze,
caught in the lid of a kerbside bin.

You walk on, then stop;
for she, this jackdaw of a woman in a sunlit street,
needs a beholder, and that is you.

> *These people*
> *rising and diving*
> *like fractious gulls*
> *intercepting prayers*
> *thriving on standing supreme*
> *over the weak*
> *the deviants and the derelicts.*

A pack of tissues (only one pound) for a passer-by,
elegant lady with Gucci shades.
A shake of the head,
a coin pressed into the palm,
a curl of the lips,
a compassionate hand laid on the old woman's shoulder,
a parting without looking back.

Now there's no-one else in the city
but you and the old woman.
And you, the voyeur, use the same light as her
but see things differently.

She draws a tissue from the unsold pack,
wipes her shoulder, cleansing the foul touch.
She steps to the kerb and stands,
Eurydice on the edge.
You recall a Hopper painting –
a woman standing like a discarded mannequin
in the window, waiting or trapped: a man, a woman, together
but not together, not wanting to be there.

> *I am hidden from the cars*
> *each full of gulls*
> *they cannot see me*
> *they cannot see*
> *my long-boned beauty*
> *my grace*
> *my poise*
> *my natural elegance.*

You imagine fingertips grip
wire netting as she looks out or in. You imagine
this part-time shop girl with the graceless manner;
mercurial director in sartorial splendour;
high-kicking chorus girl and part-time sinner;
dutiful wife spreading her legs in surrender;
a barren vessel storing silence and fears.

This sixty-year-old with one hundred years
of hand-me-down lies and withered promises,
death stalking her with the patience of a cat.

Each of these gulls
still has a name
an identity
an illusion
all are ions and atoms,
bipeds on a planet
spinning towards
its latest mass extinction –
oh the comedy of it all.

She jerks and turns,
tweaked by a playful puppeteer,
the opened pack
in her tendered hand.

You, the voyeur, look away, walk on,
feel the crack and snap of words
stuttering on your tongue.

On the Rails

At night he dreams of the sound of steam,
after grafting with men his grandfather's age.
Swamped in overalls over Superdry t-shirt,
he affects a wise expression, chain-munches

Jelly Tots as he wire-wools rust-red bolts –
a slow CPR for a loco's remains.
Playing truant from Xbox evenings,
happy to be infected by nostalgia,

he shadows drivers into the cabs,
inhales the incense of burning coals,
rubs oily cloths between his hands,
the lotion which helps to make him a man.

He knows the route, a thousand miles too short:
surgery, church, pub, the jungled garden
clawing at a broken swing. The bridge
where that family often stands – the father

and mother not at blows, their children smiling,
always. He's allowed to control the throttle
on the straight into Highley; onlookers
do their job and look on as he waves

a regal wave, senses their awe. Arm resting
on the window frame, he listens to the song
of steel on steel and the rush, rush of steam,
making clouds in a cloudless sky.

Faith in Pharmacy

Something for dreams, I say. Dreams I've had lately,
where she told me all about the knife

held to her throat in front of her child,
the clipping of her wings, the containing

of a life in a box. Surely there's a cure
in those flasks of potions, or in a drawer?

He stands with hands spread on his dark oak counter,
a backdrop of extracts: snakeroot, wormwood, plantain...

He's supposed to know exactly how to
right such ills. Do I have to fix this alone?

Give me something, I say, anything,
I'll mix it myself, to make things better.

But then he says, here's what to do –
don't dream, don't sleep, don't hope;

you know what it's like when you catch your breath?
Do that. Do that all the time.

Mrs Fortune

(inspired by Edward Hopper's 'Western Motel')

In the taxi to the hotel it was grief,
relief and guilt, an even geometry.
Then the manicured receptionist
frisked Mrs Fortune's conscience:
You booked a double room,
just for yourself is it, Madam?

Placing her overnight bag on the bed,
Mrs Fortune wonders if the curtains will meet
when drawn, for even Mr Fortune
seldom saw her unclothed,
so how can they expect a lady to disrobe
in a room where the window
is the size of a minor planet?

Does she catch a flash and glint of westering sun
on prying lenses in those hills? She stands,
touches ruly hair back into place,
brushes imaginary creases from her dress
three sizes too big for her dreams.

Softening in the brass and plush of the bath,
she neatly arrays the complimentary shampoos,
thinks of Mr Fortune in the days
before the time she doesn't mention:
his faded tartan slippers, those weary grey Y-fronts...
the days at his emotional outpost, the days
when she was merely a spectator.

Mrs Fortune orders the cheapest champagne
(to celebrate a life – he'd understand)

and from the bed she watches
the pinpoint bubbles abscond,
considers the wife, the lover,
she might have been. A satin X
in a queen-size bed.

Later, as she draws the curtains,
inspecting the seams for precision,
an ink-blot spider with wide-lens eyes and bony legs
scuttles across her outstretched hand.
She screams and flaps, shakes
and sobs behind the bathroom door.
Closing her eyes, she aches
for the late Mr Fortune to share
her romantic weekend for one.

The Triumph of Uncertainty

This is a world where doors cannot be closed
for ever. Where the view from the gate
is filled by a mountain, daubed in pastel grey,
footed by the softly raging river.
This is a world where I am young and I am old,
where my legs can bear my weight
yet will often give way
when least expected. It's the weight
that makes it so unsure, so tiring.
And half-way up the spiral staircase, a window
sill with an oyster-pink orchid.
Now the blooms are ready
to drop, they've done their job;
if I watch and wait, new buds will follow
but I cannot guarantee it.
From the upstairs room
I see a world where fog or cloud
come and go at will. And, listen, the muffled
voices beyond these walls, talking in a rhythm,
words I can't make out, spoken
at half-speed, low and threatening,
treacherous, giving me nothing in return.
And halfway down the spiral staircase,
a window sill with an oyster-pink orchid, in bloom.

Children in the Presence of Snow

On this day, the stuff has been delivered
in quantity and consistency
for the creation of an acting deity.

If we had real eyes we'd use them,
but for now two pebbles will do;
a pair of old specs driven hard into the head.

It's not until the implanting
of the Hula Hoop mouth
with its startled O

that we begin to imagine
the waft of gin on its breath
and a vexed *please get me out of here.*

Our veneration is cut short by a slow
easy thaw, saving a kicking
by a neighbour's prickly child,

or the embellishment of pert white breasts
by the bawdy wag across the road
in an onset of boredom,

or the chance of going to war
with the unworthies
over our indivisible creation.

The Last of the Covington Blackberries

Now, she sees the blackberries in monochrome
without the purple lustre.

She recalls their village hedgerows being thorny,
and how he fussed about the cuts and scratches.

After a glass or two of wine she stood
in their kitchen, holding up each swollen fruit

as if a treasured jewel, counting the drupelets,
checking nature's work, slurring the numbers

and giggling when he mumbled some remark
on madness running in her family.

Later, she searched online for 'blackberries' and 'secrets'
– *Fight mild infection, anti-tumour; easy to freeze...*

Six months on, there's a crumble to be made,
enough thawed fruit for one. His loss, her fate:

she's better off alone; he'll crawl back
but it will be too late. The blackberries

are black, and she could take you now
to the hedgerow where they grew

and you'd help her check for dried blood
on the stems and you wouldn't say a word

as she drags her fist amongst the thorns
again and again and again.

In the Museum of Air Guitars

It's free, take the time of your life. Start
with your first air guitar, acoustic,
virtually made from the last elm in the land;
nothing fancy, sound-hole shaped
like a heart. Relive how you'd slacken
and tighten the pegs as you sat on your stool
in your bootleg depiction of cool.

This was truly escape, to feel the echo
rollick so freely in the chamber,
a welcome release for someone
raised on a diet of silent rebuke.

Move to the next, a Rickenbacker
with its gold-leafed whammy bar,
the heel of your hand would lick it
like there's no hope of a tomorrow.
An instrument for standing, turning,
raising dust on the living room floor.
You'd arc the head, feel the scorch,
tap the toe of your snakeskin boots

but when you stopped to take a bow
there was no-one to applaud
and no-one to be dismayed.

Then, the supreme of supremes,
the platinum Fender with silver frets,
the one you played for the President
who wept over your octave-busting
rendition of My Wildest Dreams:
let the eagle fly, soar higher and higher,

through the ceiling, through that rainbow,
up to the stars, your biggest dream

until jarred back by your tether:
you never learn
never have done, never will.

The Other Me

Too far away there's another town
with another me and another you
and the other me says what he thinks
and winks at girls when the other you
is at his side;
he knows he's the dog's,
the man with the rod, the bare-chested god
who struts and strides, tick-tocks into lives,
nurtures the moods, wouldn't think twice
about hitching a ride or raising a fist
or slugging a mate, boozed up or not,
he's as slick as a knife in the gut

     and the other you
is you
     and the other me
is him
     and I was tricked into
     not being me
     so I reach out to you
     reach out to you
     over and over
     and over again
but you're too far away
you've always been
too far away

Cut-price Cut

My barber's name is Frank –
he has kind hands, a kinder heart
as he charges me mates' rates.
I sit in the chair, he capes me up
and always says, *Hello Jim*
despite my name being John,
but I daren't tell him, as Johns
may not get the discount.
Before he gets in first, I ask him
Going anywhere nice this year?
and he says, *Magaluf, so no. How about you, Jim?*
as he clips and snips, runs his busy buzzy trimmer
down the back of my neck in a surprisingly sensual way.
I say, *Skegness,*
though in truth we're off to one of our villas in Bermuda
on our second-best yacht
but that might scupper the mates' rates.
Ah, Skeggy! He runs his fingers through my hair
in a final gesture of barberhood. *The missus and me*
own three hotels there. You'll have to drop in –
mates' rates, just for you, Jim.
He whips the cape off me, matador-style,
and I think of leaving a tip
but don't.

50

Hair Loss: The Musical

It opens with second-glancing the mirror
turning my back with a deluded shrug
      tra la la

I get sentimental about a hair
      found tunnelling in my paella
la la la   *te-dum te-dum*

I compose a list of 20 creative ways
      to up-cycle scarpered strands
      woo hoo   woo hoo

and now 'Involuntary Deforestation'
a wistful ballad in 3/4 time
      tra la la   *tra la la*

they say my fossil-smooth arena can be seen from space
big enough for a nuthatch to skate the Bolero
      la la la la dum te dum

but it's fine to rue my hair withering on the barber's floor
      real fine
          no, really really fine
    be-doo-be wop wop

cheer up   *cheer up*
see the fancy eloquence of dancers
hear the whimsical thigh-slapping song
      paying homage to rug-makers and milliners
          weavers and grafters
    wop   *wop*   *doo-wop*

the ultimate distraction before the curtain falls
encore   encore

meanwhile the world still spins
and the hum and thrum of the stage
      tells me that hope without hair is okay
        be-doo-be wop wop

and I sit on the edge
clutch a hairbrush
        bristling with memories
       doo-be wop wop
     dreaming of you

A Duck in the Lounge

We have a duck in the lounge at home,
it's very much the elephant in the room
as we never ever talk about it,
except at Christmas when we plan the festive menu.

Where it came from and how it got there
we don't know. It waddles about,
we step over or around it. Sometimes
it quacks and flaps its wings,
this elephant in the room,
but we don't want to respond
to the attention-seeking.

It craps quite a lot, harder to ignore,
and we have to explain to guests
that it's not our doing,
it belongs to the elephant in the room,
and they just nod, smile, then talk
a little too quickly about the weather.

We have a duck in the lounge at home,
it's very much the elephant in the room.

Hasn't it been a lovely summer?

The Door Man

He collects doors like others collect stamps,
catalogues them by wood and style and shade;
he can tell you their Janka hardness
if you only dare stay a while. He ran

out of space in the house, fazed the guests
who couldn't tell collection doors from those
they could use to move from room to room.
He wept at a split on a light oak Shaker,

as did his wife of eighteen years
when he dumped her for a maple louvre.
She was never for him, with her ludicrous array
of hinges and bolts that cluttered the place,

and her baffling tolerance of uPVC.
These days, he dines off a knotty pine bi-fold,
watches TV with a flush beech at his side,
breathes sweet nothings through the keyhole

of a demi softwood French. He sleeps alone
on a Brazilian teak, dreams of finding
a cedar half-glaze on a skip in the street,
or the love of a collector of locks and latches.

He will not recall why he sets the blaze;
he will watch from the safety of the local park
as all but the fireproofs turn to ash.

Den, Sole Occupancy

I built a den in the living room, just for me.
Minimalist design, mainly blankets and sheets
draped over curtain poles and a golf club.

In the glimmer of a fading Maglite
it's the echoless drear of autumn in here,
not enough room for a solitary tango
or a quick-fire round of celebrity charades.

I lie on my back, feeling weightless,
stare at the astral alignment of the buttons on her coat,
which doubles as the makeshift door. Now
on with the headphones, so the noise is less black.
Invent a new game – count the buttons on the coat.
See a new something – one blonde hair,
caught in the thread of the button at the end.
Create a new plan – build a den within a den,
then another, and another, and another,
until the last is as small as a jackdaw's egg.

I'd invite you in, I could unhitch the coat
from the golf club. But we'd only mess it up.

The Parable of the Peahen in the Close

We could have shot it, bludgeoned it to death,
or chased it, teased it, caught it, plucked it bald.

We chose to stand and watch from the road
as the peahen, unfazed by our presence
and a stranger to suburbia, stalked
amongst the nurtured flowerbeds next door.

There were two, then four, then twelve of us,
a gathering of neighbours from our close,
sharing knowledge, exchanging morsels
of peahen facts and misinformation.

Some complained; they would have liked
the bronze and green of a male's fanned train
with scores of eyes, not this dismal plumage
and the merest hint of iridescence.

The multitude moved from garden to garden,
following the bird and swelling our ranks.
By the top of the close we were sixty
or more, residents of several years

babbling to those who had barely earned
a nod or a wave from a passing car.
Names were exchanged, promises of dinner
dates, weekend outings and barbecues.

A church warden from number sixty-six
appeared with a plate of fish finger sarnies,
not enough to go round it seemed to me
but, to the wonderment of all, it did.

A brawl broke out and two men scrapped
about a wife being somewhat less than faithful.
The IT geek from eighty-nine tasered one
in the crotch then coyly announced

that he has a way with gadgets, while the spinster
in black from that house with a name,
played whale sounds from a tape deck held aloft
to calm things down a bit, and informed us

that the peahen was a sign of the end of the world.
Heads down, we hurried to our homes,
gathered our children close, and kept watch
from the safety of upstairs windows.

No-one knew where and when the peahen went,
some thought they'd imagined it, a vision,
until photos on our phones showed the beauty
of that merest hint of iridescence.

An account of the last moments of the poet

When I take the wrong turn and find myself
clomping up the steps to the block,
take my word, it's not what I want to do –
a bloody inconvenient way to go.
I'm lost for words until the chap in black,
axe in hand, sporting a dog-collar for a laugh,
enquires with a growl *any last request?*

Always the chancer, I ask to phone Childline,
even though I'm nearly forty-two. Maybe
some muscle rub, to ease my aching limbs?
Saxophone lessons I've always yearned for. If not,
I'll settle for flute. And there's a Mills & Boon
I've got to finish. I've started to descale my kettle,
yet another job half-done. Now I'm asking
for a traybake as all the excitement
is making me peckish. I'd love a book
on mindfulness and an aspirin or two
for this mother of a migraine.
And maybe a tetanus shot, just in case?

When I request Axeman to join me
for a selfie he starts to get grouchy
and makes me kneel.
Still, I'm chuffed to see that the audience is good,
biggest crowd for a gig in years;
one or two ladies are knitting –
that's what poetry does to some.
As I lay down my head, the traybake turns up,
a miracle too late, but poetry fans love their lemon drizzle.

It's when I hear the slice and swish of the axe

that my self-doubt fades, a long-awaited new poem
with long vowels and a happy ending rushes
into my head just as I see bloody stars
and smears of kindly light float
through the weave of the basket.

Shush now,
shush.

Death of a Guiltmonger

The chugger lies at my feet, still
conscious after the beating I gave him —
this is what you get when you stalk

the high street with your clipboard
and demand a minute of someone's time.
I'm not too keen on being mugged for charity

and haven't given him the chance
to name the noble cause:
Syria, Africa, dogs or donkeys,

or maybe orphaned wasps.
I can tell in his eyes that his own funds
come first, no doubt for a trip to Prague.

I nudge him in the ribs for luck
with the toe of my Jimmy Choo loafer.
He's making a fuss, uncharitable curses

hissing through broken teeth.
I'm in a rush: every second I'm here
a child is dying, a family bombed,

donkeys whipped by a Bolivian farmer's hoe,
a juvenile wasp's mummy and daddy
barbarically squashed underfoot.

I stoop at his side and wrench the pen
away from his twitching hand.
Quick, show me where to sign.

He points to the page then passes out,
leaves traces of his blood
smeared across the dotted line.

I walk away, it's done: two quid a month
to the Home for Battered Chuggers.
I can hold my head up high.

The Piano Tuner

So much in here
in here
reads
he how)

The twilit alcove in the Front Room
hugged our old upright piano. Every spring

the tuner called, tapped his way to the stool,
laid down his white stick and lifted the lid.
Mother moved the Toby Jug off the top,

just in case. Staring ahead, as if he could read
clefs, rests and accidentals in the wood grain,

he hummed a note, settled a finger on a key,
sensed a stray dot of sawdust balanced
on a lever, or the middling thud of a string

that had forgotten its calling. With the attention
of a fighter pilot on a mission, he coaxed

the sound from within, eyes closed
as though it made a difference. From a low
angle I watched as he tested the scales,

giving them what-for, notes tumbling around me
like a rain shower after a dry spell or snow

on Christmas morning. I always wanted to ask
if his eyes were pecked out by starlings or
if being too good at something might make us blind.

Mother busied herself with pointless
dusting of ornaments, smiled uncertainly

when he turned his head in her direction.
And after he tapped his way out of the house,
she'd place the Toby Jug back on top,

close the lid over the keys for another year.

Numbers

Inside it must be as it was; surely
they wouldn't be so thoughtless and change
her childhood home. The numbers on the door
are the same (why does that surprise her?)
but tarnished now, screws with many years of rust.

She stands with her back to the door, takes in the view:
parking for three where the roses stood guard;
the spot where she found the seagull carcass.
Then, she'd looked for hours
at the glimpse of sea between the hills,
thinking she could hear pebbles on the beach
clatter beneath the receding waves.
Now, there's a building in the way, its brash neon sign
reflects orange on the slick of the street.

It unsettles her. Does she still want to see inside?
Her father is not at home; he won't be greeting
with the crackle of that antique radio.
Her mother is not at home; she won't be greeting
with the reek of overcooked meat.

Here is her father, standing tall at her side
on a summer evening, sharing the last
of the sun going down:
he's pulling on his cigarette,
she's clutching her favourite doll.
She wonders if he's tired again,
yet he finds the strength to pick her up
and they watch the glimpse of sea together,
her cheek pressed hard to his.
The glow of his cigarette, the same colour as the sun;

the smoke makes her eyes water.
I love these sunsets, he says. *Don't you?*

Yes, I do. She brushes her fingertips
over the tarnished numbers,
more treasured than a Saxon hoard.

Man On

(observations on watching an amateur soccer game)

Man on! It's Three over there,
in the blue on the line, only half
his thoughts on the ball as he leafs
through images: high-speed trains
and creosoted sheds, pausing at Sadie
sipping her Lambrusco and wanting
to do it again in the back of his Astra
on the way home from the bank.

Language, lads! This from the man in black.

Man on! No, not Five! He's a man never on.
He jogs into space, then rocks
and smirks like an only-child waiting
on the doorstep. Bloody glaciers. Discovery Channel
gives him nightmares. Jellyfish next week. Or sea anemones.
Whatever. Marine invertebrates with their radically
symmetrical bodies, they're the worst.

Man on! Poaching eggs in heaven is Four,
standing with his back to the steeple,
riding the seven hills, he's the man
in a suit who knocks on doors, flogs
his faith, tugs at shirts, dreams
of Eccles cakes and occasional bouts
of ever-so-judicious pornography
behind dusty velvet curtains.

Come on lads, be nice! This from the man in black.

Man on! It's Nine – there he goes,
running like sheep piss through bracken,
sinking under the boot of a full-bodied Red.
Bury him where he fell: one of nature's best,
the uncaressed, the amicable one
whose sweet peas are the talk of The Close.
A valiant end for a languid fullback,
fleshy as an overstuffed toy, and now
doing a Lazarus for the pensive fan
with the half-finished Daily Mail crossword.

Man on! It won't be the goalie,
digging at divots, stealing a glance
at the pigtailed girl on the touchline.
Picked for width over skill, he's dying
for a ciggie but daren't light up
until the half-time whistle. He kicks
the post with a heel, thinking of his ex,
and what he'll find to do with his kids
on Sunday. Pizza and the flicks, again.

Man on! And the man is Seven,
everyone's pal, cap and bells,
the one who dares, elbows high,
dried blood on his studs;
a muted soldier marking time,
pulling the guy off the bonfire
to become his best friend. All good thoughts
should have an apostrophe
in the world-according-to-Seven.

Come on, lads, play fair! This from the man in black,
the twister and yanker, the striker at home,
(stopping just short of arterial blood)

the silhouette on the creaking stairs,
the love-is-never-saying-sorry official,
training the inner killer. The end,
when it comes, will be slow,
no doubt after extra time
and a crowd-pleasing shoot-out.

Marzipan

I cannot kill the marzipan man,
he has no heart, no lung, no brain –
a hardened paste of almonds and sugar,
part of the marzipan crowd
with their tabloid thoughts.

I could prick him with a needle,
see him wince, writhe and curse;
I ought to test his nakedness,
not waste that moment
when he's bound to beg for mercy.

Yet others do love him, worship
the ground he stands on, treat him well,
graffiti his name on subway walls,
enjoy his sour taste, tell us he's harmless
and greatly misunderstood.

I know better; this shape-shifter
can charm and enchant, call the shots
in this game of power.
Maybe I should do the deed,
as a gift to mankind,
and tear him limb from limb.

Numbers in Gold

When he was a boy, he would jot down
the numbers on buses – four digits stencilled
in gold by the doors. He would sit on the wall
by the flyover in rain or sun; drivers
and conductors waved, gave the thumbs up,
a sign to show their one-ness. A sprint of a bike ride
to the terminus, where all the buses slept,
could harvest a dozen or more fresh ones:
new livery, new style, new fleet,
an outing of note, for a while.

These days he has to squint to read
the numbers as they surge past in the traffic.
He's more likely to recite the long-range
weather forecast than a list of types of bus.
A trudge to the terminus ends with holding back
tears while he peers into the building,
one hand on the doorframe
as he dodges the wary glances
of the granite-faced drivers.

He stops to catch his breath on the way home,
wets himself just twenty steps from his gate;
he's spent too long out. Later,
he pulls his edge-worn Woolworths notebook
from a drawer, reminds himself
of the make and model for each number
listed in a neat school-essay hand.
Looking up from his armchair,
through the half-net curtained window,
he can see the tops of buses ghost by,
skimming the jagged horizon of the fence:

red roof, heads and shoulders of passengers
wrapped in solitary shadows.

A horn bellows with invisible ferocity and he imagines
it was meant for him. From the book, clipped
keepsake tickets in old-money pence
scatter onto his lap; he rubs one
between finger and thumb,
as if trying to release the moment.

(↑ School)

REPORT:
Maths 31% English 89% History 78% Art 63%

> *he is a pleasant pupil*
> *his exam results are somewhat better*
> *than even the most pessimistic teacher expected*

Miss Wardle tries hard to be
a Bastard of the First Order
factors, fractions, integrals, integers,
angles, octals, rationals, irrationals
lessons in Maths Humiliation again today.

> *he needs to listen more to his teacher*
> *he often loses concentration*
> *and that affects his work*

I wish a near-death experience
upon her, repeat one hundred times;
see her stare as she draws my blood.

> *he needs to develop his communication skills*
> *he doesn't talk much*

She advances:

You, what is x plus y?

Her pinched cheeks, ivory, close enough to claw;
her quink-black eyes, close enough to skewer
with my newly sharpened HB pencil.

We both wait for something to happen:
x plus y – it's twenty-two – if I try to say it

my stammer will make her laugh again.

t - t - t
ha-ha-ha
t - t - twenty-t-t-t
all together now children
ha-ha-ha
ha-ha-ha

> *he doesn't seem confident in any subject*
> *needs to improve a lot*
> how we don't know
> and, of course, we don't give a fuck

I often wondered

about the shape of Mother's Worry

was it
runaway-bus-shaped
      girlfriend's-blush-shaped
            unmuzzled-dog-shaped
      class-A-drug-shaped
underage-sex-shaped
      overage-sex-shaped
            office-rumour-shaped
      hide-and-seek-tumour-shaped

but no

it was shaped
like an endless row of reluctant ampersands
      & & & & & & & &
squatting   poised   to be sent into combat
one by one

The boy who couldn't say his name

They ask his name, their faces masks of hate
or dumbness. And when the word doesn't come
they round on him and kick him down
'ere, woss yer name? yer stupid, yer dimwit,
s'only yer name, only yer name...

He's in the game of seek-and-chide,
caught up in their way of killing time;
their joke, their bond, their fix,
stop him dead in his tracks,
the hunters, the hunted, taunt him till he cries
oh, 'e can cry all right
slap him on his back as if he were an infant choking
come on, spit it out, woss yer name?

They'd ripped out his heart long ago,
ground his bones, drank his blood,
peeled his skin, ate his brain,
turned his body into fodder,
fed his tongue to the baying crowds.

He knows he can whisper his name
when alone; it makes the journey
from shadow to light on broken breath –
he thinks that odd as he unclips the watch
from his wrist, and takes a long hard look.

Cornet Player on the Run

Guilty. I deserted from the Salvation Army
halfway through Onward Christian Soldiers –
uniformed, second cornet, first-rate sinner,
part of a circle deployed outside Safeway's.
Somewhere between a perfect B flat
and a truncated C sharp
I decided to detach.
Roy on trombone and Pete on bass drum
fluffed decoy notes and beats
as I stepped back into enemy lines.

Merging with the grocery-laden infidels,
I dropped down on one knee
looking this way and that, coiled
like a spring, cornet at the ready,
sweeping an arc. Shedding my cap, running low,
light on my feet, on my toes, through the doors,
commando crawl through Snacks and Treats –
no cry of *Deserter*! no cry of *Backslider*!
no volley of *Hallelujahs*
no thump-thump-thump
of chasing boots, no slingshot
searing past my ear, no jangle
of incoming tambourines.

Kneeling in a corner, flushed, faithless,
I stayed until dark, praying
not to be found.

Frost Flower

Do not try and use this to persuade,
to mourn, or for love: ice blossoms
will disappoint an intake of breath.

Within the clarity of cut glass
there is no stamen, style nor stigma
on these day-shy blooms.

A touch before sunrise
shatters petals into diamonds
or glistens your fingertip.

Tomorrow you will sit, watching
flowers on the stalks that died
a week ago or more; you will listen

to the white-on-white rhythm
of winter, hear the crackle
of cold in the ribbons of ice.

UnBreaking

i)

Sometimes a heart can break.
Not dropped on an unyielding tile-hard floor
to shatter into gem-sized fragments
Not splintered into the knife-blade-thickness
of rifts in unseasoned kindling
Not like the unearthing of a pit of bones
all with fractures from soldiers' rifle-butts
Not bread broken into mass-sized pieces
for a line of Sunday half-believers
Not the clean snap of a KitKat bar
between the V of ungloved hands
Not the cracking of a pensioner's skull
with a baseball bat from JD Sports
Not the curtain of night-cloud parting
for a glimpse of the moon's borrowed sunlight
Not the unisoned break-down of black-clad mourners
as their loved one finishes dying.

ii)

Sometimes a heart can break, but no,
not suddenly like that – a heart can break
like the crazing lines on a fire-glazed vase,
where the *ping* of the creeping fractures
goes on and on for ever. A muttered *no*,
a lingering *so what*, a flicker of hate
in a sideways glance, the unworn ridge
in the middle of the bed, the days
of making-do and the nights of fake-believe;
two trapped half-lives, no longer a whole.

iii)

Maybe, sometimes, things can unbreak –
the kindling and the rifle-butts and the baseball bat
are restored to a tree and the dead wake back to life
and in my dream of all dreams you can't wait
to break the silence with an i-love-you;
yes, I want more of you and you want more of me
and in every crazy day together
there's a carnival of things unbroken.
Sometimes, a heart can unbreak. Maybe.

John Lawrence lives in Worcestershire, although he was born and (some say) bred in the Black Country. He gave up a career in IT Consultancy to gain a BA in Creative Writing at the University of Birmingham, where he 'found' poetry. A popular respected poet and performer, he loves writing poems that are entertaining and unsettling at the same time, making the reader think, without being wilfully obscure. His work is informed by family, experience, his roots in a Salvation Army household, and ever-present doubts about why we are here. John's parody *The Secret Five and the Stunt Nun Legacy* (Matador, 2010) is powered by the same imaginative wit as his poetry. *The boy who couldn't say his name* is his first poetry collection.

V.